W9-CCO-198

This story is dedicated to my five children—my stars.
We all have an opportunity to be flexible, to expand our vision, and to put love first.
Thank you for helping me see more, do more, and love more.
—J.P.

To my Dadda Ladda Myles C. Pinkney
—C.P.B.

Text copyright © 2021 by Jodie Patterson
Jacket art and interior illustrations copyright © 2021 by Charnelle Pinkney Barlow

All rights reserved. Published in the United States by Crown Books for Young Readers, an imprint of
Random House Children's Books, a division of Penguin Random House LLC, New York.

Crown and the colophon are registered trademarks of Penguin Random House LLC.

Visit us on the Web! rhcbooks.com

Educators and librarians, for a variety of teaching tools,
visit us at RHTeachersLibrarians.com

Library of Congress Cataloging-in-Publication Data
Names: Patterson, Jodie, author. | Pinkney Barlow, Charnelle, illustrator.
Title: Born ready : the true story of a boy named Penelope / Jodie Patterson, Charnelle Pinkney Barlow.
Description: First edition. | New York : Crown Books for Young Readers, 2021. | Audience: Ages 4–8. | Audience: Grades K–1. |
Summary: Just before his fifth birthday, Penelope lets his mother know he is a boy and, with her support and his ninja powers,
faces the rest of his family and his classmates. Drawn from the author's memoir, The bold world.
Identifiers: LCCN 2020010665 (print) | LCCN 2020010666 (ebook) | ISBN 978-0-593-12363-8 (hardcover) |
ISBN 978-0-593-12365-2 (library binding) | ISBN 978-0-593-12364-5 (ebook)
Subjects: CYAC: Transgender people—Fiction. | Family life—Fiction. | African Americans—Fiction.
Classification: LCC PZ7.1.P3814 Bor 2021 (print) | LCC PZ 7.1.P3814 (ebook) | DDC [E]—dc23

The text of this book is set in 14-point Filson Pro.
The illustrations in this book were created digitally with handmade watercolor textures.
Book design by Nicole de las Heras

Printed in the United States of America
10 9 8 7 6 5 4 3 2 1
First Edition

Random House Children's Books supports the First Amendment and celebrates the right to read.

BORN READY

THE TRUE STORY OF A BOY NAMED PENELOPE

Written by
JODIE PATTERSON

Illustrated by
Charnelle Pinkney Barlow

Crown Books for Young Readers ♛ New York

I'm no ordinary kid. I'm a ninja.

Ninjas are strong. Ninjas are smart. Ninjas always win the fight. Usually, ninjas have ninja names.

But my parents named me after my grandmother Penelope. And that makes things hard.

Penelope, you're so cute! Penelope, you look like your sister! No one understands.

Big Brother acts like he knows everything.

"Penelope, do you know that the air around a lightning bolt is hotter than the sun?"

"Nope."

"Do you know that everything has a scientific explanation?"

"Nope."

I may not know everything. But I know what I like. Skateboards and high-tops, baggy blue jeans, button-front shirts, math, science, and getting straight A's. And most of all, a Mohawk haircut—pleeeease!

Mama is the busiest person I know.
Papa is the strongest person I know.
Big Brother is the smartest.
Big Sister is the bossiest.
And Baby, he's the happiest—he can make anyone smile.

If they'd all stop and listen, I'd tell them about me. Inside I'm a boy.

When I close my eyes and dream, I'm a boy.

When I karate-chop the bad guys, I. Am. A. Boy.

But my family is too busy to notice.

I stomp through the house
so they HEAR me.

I cut the line at the playground so they SEE me.

I pound my fists hard so they FEEL me.

"Time out! Pleppy, why are you so angry?" Mama asks.

"Because everyone thinks I'm a girl."

"However you feel is fine, baby. It's what's on the inside that matters most. If you feel like a boy, that's okay."
"No, Mama, I don't *feel* like a boy. I AM a boy."

"Oh?"

Mama gets quiet.

"I love you, Mama, but I don't want to *be* you. I want to be Papa. I don't want tomorrow to come because tomorrow I'll look like you. Please help me, Mama. Help me be a boy."

I hold Mama's hand and transfer some of my ninja powers to help her understand.

Then Mama says the best word I've ever heard.
"Yes."
She says, "We will make a plan to tell everyone we love what we know."
"What's that?"
"You are a boy."

For the first time, my insides don't feel like fire.
They feel like warm, golden love.

Our family is from all over the world, and Mama says that makes us wise.

Grandpa G flies from Ghana for my birthday.

Mama bakes a cake.

We gather around the table.

"Akwaaba!" says Mama. "Penelope is not a pretend boy or a tomboy. He is our five-year-old big boy."

All eyes are stuck on me.

Grandpa G slams his hand down on the table. "Ah! Chale! In my language of Twi, gender isn't such a big deal. We don't use gender pronouns."

I don't understand everything, but I do know Grandpa G is smiling.

Good! Let's eat cake.

But Big Brother isn't smiling. He looks mad.

"This doesn't make sense. You can't *become* a boy. You have to be born one."

Mama puts her arms around both of us and pulls us in tight. "Not everything *needs* to make sense. *This is about love,*" she whispers.

Papa stands up tall.

"Well, P, if you want *me* to call you a boy, you'll have to tell me yourself."

I stand up tall, too. "I *am* a boy."

It's Monday, and Mama says school is my responsibility.
I'm going to show my friends all of me.

I put on my blue pants.

I button my favorite shirt.

I tighten my long tie.

I feel *good*.

I walk into school like I "own the joint"—just like Grandpa JohnnyBoy, from Harlem, taught me.

"Hey, Pen, why are you wearing a boy's uniform?" my friend Big D asks.

"Because I *am* a boy. And I like my full name, please—Penelope."

"Yeah, makes sense. And you look great," he says.

We high-five.

Principal asks to see me.

"Penelope, I heard your classmates were asking about your uniform," she says. "Were you embarrassed?"

I want to tell Principal that ninjas don't get embarrassed—we "get busy." But I just shake my head no.

"Your parents told me you are a boy. Is that true?"
"I think like a boy. I feel like a boy. I might look different from other boys, but yes, I'm sure I'm a boy."

"Well, Penelope . . . today you're *my* teacher!"

Mama says ninjas need to be powerful, so I study karate.

"Lil P, you ready for this?" Master Bill asks.

He's the loudest man I know. And I like it! He teaches me how to fight and train hard with my team.

"Lil P, give me a left foot roundhouse kick!" Master Bill says.

I try my best, but it's confusing.

"Nooooo. Your LEFT foot! Left!"

Master Bill says: If you don't *do,* you can't *become.*

Mama says: Winners are losers who get back up.

I say: Ninjas don't quit.

I practice every day.
Breathing and stretching.
Blocking and punching.

Most important, I learn to get back up.
Master Bill says I'm ready.

Papa drives us to my first tournament.
I bring my cheering squad!
"Baby, are you sure you want to fight?" Mama asks.
"Remember to protect yourself," Papa says.
"Don't worry," I tell them. "I'm not afraid."
Then Big Brother jumps in. "Ninjas never back down
from a challenge, P. You got this," he says.

When we check in at the front desk,
my teammates are already there!
"Yo! You ready, P?"
"Born ready!"

My opponent is tall.
My opponent is fast.
We've both come to win.

This won't be easy.

I shuffle my feet.
I bob from side to side.
Boom! Roundhouse kick to the head.

I score.

I win.

When they give out the gold, what
name will they call?

"And the gold goes to . . ."

"PENELOPE!"

Me.

It's my time.

I'M A BOY NAMED PENELOPE!